French Pistols
and Sporting Guns

A N Kennard FSA

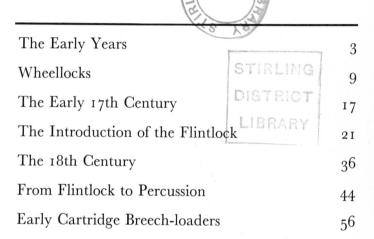

COUNTRY LIFE COLLECTORS' GUIDES

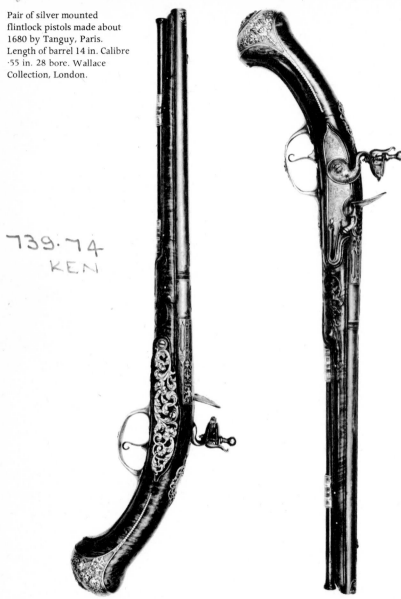

Pair of silver mounted
flintlock pistols made about
1680 by Tanguy, Paris.
Length of barrel 14 in. Calibre
·55 in. 28 bore. Wallace
Collection, London.

739·74
KEN

The Early Years

Numbers in the margin refer to the page where an illustration may be found

Little or nothing is known of the origins of gunmaking in France and the number of weapons definitely of French make which can be dated before 1550 is exceedingly small. The industry appears to have been subject in its early years to German rather than Italian influence, possibly because the trade routes to the lands of Germanic culture were physically easier of access than those lying further to the south, and up to a period around 1580 German design is apparent in French firearms both in their mechanism and in their decoration.

It is usual, indeed almost essential, for any general work on firearms to be divided up by the need to deal with the ignition systems in a certain order, and following the usual custom matchlock arms will be taken first, though this does not in the case of French firearms imply that where fine quality weapons are concerned the **matchlock** was in general use before the wheel-lock – indeed the opposite seems to have been the case. Utilitarian military weapons fitted with matchlocks must have been produced in France, as in other countries, from the mid 15th century but it is not intended in this work to deal with military weapons and only those made for private use will be considered. In fact matchlock guns characteristically French in design did not make their appearance before the last quarter of the 16th century.

The **typical French matchlock** has a most individual appearance due to the shape of the butt which has a pronounced downward curve. It is also quite thick and has no 'small', i.e.

3

it does not become more slender at the beginning of the butt proper to make it easier to grip with the trigger-hand. This curved shape results in the butt being quite short, and since it obviously cannot be placed against the shoulder of the firer some writers in the past have stated that it is intended to be placed against the chest. Since, however, many of these guns are provided with backsights such a position would be quite impractical since with the butt held against the chest the firer's head could not be lowered sufficiently for his eye to register with the sight, and there is little doubt that the guns were in fact held with the butt against the cheek in the firing position. The

Matchlock gun of about 1570–1580. Length of barrel 50·5 in. Calibre ·73 in. 12 bore. Armouries, Tower of London.

Matchlock gun of about 1570–1580. Armouries, Tower of London.

Matchlock gun of about 1570–1580. Metropolitan Museum of Art, New York (gift of William H. Riggs, 1913).

Matchlock gun of about 1575 with gold and silver damascening. Length of barrel 25·4 in. Calibre ·44 in. 54 bore. Armouries, Tower of London.

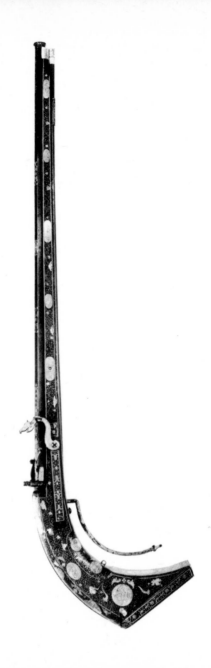

triggers fitted to these French matchlocks have a very characteristic form, being long and slender, curved to follow the shape of the underside of the butt. One end of the trigger is screwed into the sear, the other having a small acorn-shaped finial. Since the triggers are simply screwed into the tail of the sear and have a tendency to become unscrewed, they are prevented from doing this by being slipped through a cord loop fastened to a small ring which is fixed to the underside of the butt.

There is nothing characteristically French about the locks fitted to weapons of this type; they are of an international pattern and consist of a long, narrow, rectangular lockplate on the inner side of which is mounted a long sear, pivoted in the centre, to one end of which is attached the trigger, the other end being linked to the arbor of the match-holder or serpentine in such a manner that upward pressure on the trigger brings the serpentine holding the glowing match downwards into the priming-pan. A spring bears against the sear and keeps the serpentine raised until depressed into the firing position.

The barrels fitted to these matchlocks are long and slender, the first third of the length from the breech end usually being of octagonal section, often fluted, while there is frequently a moulding at the muzzle on which the foresight is mounted, the backsight, when present, being generally of tubular peepsight form. The stock decoration usually consists of inlays of bone or stag-horn shaped and engraved as animals and human figures, an exception being the **beautiful little gun** in the Armouries, Tower of London, where the stock decoration consists of foliage inlaid in brass wire, interspersed with engraved plaques of mother-of-pearl, the barrel, lock and heel-plate of the butt being encrusted with decoration in silver and gold of a peculiarly French type. The French style of matchlock gun was mainly produced in Northern France and was used in Flanders as well as in its country of origin.

Weapons with matchlock ignition were not made in France after the first ten years of the 17th century but a few **very late specimens** differ from those just mentioned in having straighter butts intended to be placed against the shoulder.

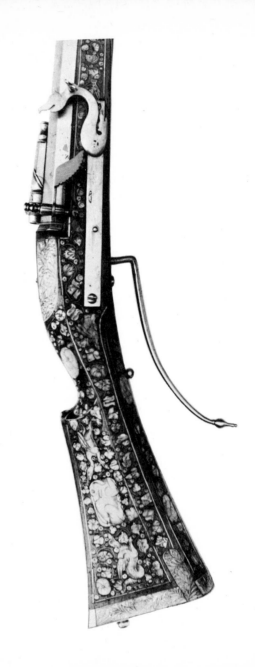

French or Flemish matchlock gun of about 1590–1600. Nederlands Legermuseum, Leiden.

Wheellocks

The latest researches show that the wheellock was probably invented in Italy in the first decade of the 16th century, examples soon being imported into Germany, where the mechanism was being produced by the 1520s.

10, 62 The **wheellock** is a somewhat complicated mechanism. Briefly, it consists of a wheel placed flat on the outer side of a lockplate and mounted on an arbor or axle which passes through the plate, where it is connected by a short chain to a strong V-shaped mainspring. The outer end of the wheel-arbor is squared for a key or spanner and the lock is spanned by winding the wheel through three-quarters of a revolution, when the nose of the sear penetrates a hole drilled in the lockplate and falls into a recess in the inner side of the wheel. Mounted on the lockplate, usually in front of but occasionally behind the wheel, is a pivoted arm or doghead provided with a spring and corresponding to the serpentine of the matchlock, though in this case provided with jaws in which are clamped a piece of iron pyrites. When the lock is to be fired the doghead is brought over so that the pyrites makes contact with the edge of the wheel, which protrudes into the bottom of the priming-pan through a slot. Pressure on the trigger withdraws the sear from the recess in the wheel, which revolves briefly but at high speed, striking sparks from the pyrites which ignite the priming-powder in the pan. The priming-powder was retained in the pan by a sliding pan-cover which was closed either manually or, in the case of the earlier French wheellocks, by a spring with a press-button release. It was possible to bring the doghead into the firing position with the pyrites resting on the closed pan-cover. When the sear was withdrawn and the wheel revolved, a cam on the wheel-arbor struck an arm attached to the pan-cover and knocked it back, thus allowing the doghead holding the pyrites to descend into the pan and make contact with the wheel. It will be understood from the above description that the wheellock was a complicated and expensive piece of mechanism, but it was not unreliable if kept clean and in good order. It was a great improvement on the matchlock which, although having the merits of simplicity and cheapness, required constant attention on the part of the user to keep the smouldering match clamped in the serpentine to the right length, while in wet weather the difficulty of keeping it alight was very considerable indeed.

The introduction of the wheellock made the manufacture of pistols practical, since a weapon fitted with this form of ignition could be carried in saddle-holsters or in the belt, if necessary even with the lock spanned, since the pan-cover over the priming-powder prevented accidental discharge. Pistols fitted with matchlocks were never made in western Europe, or, if made, have not survived to the present day.

Mechanism of carbine (opposite).

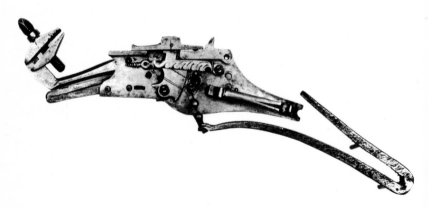

There is little doubt that the wheellock was introduced into France from Germany, possibly by way of Flanders, the earliest dated weapon exhibiting any French characteristics being a **short carbine** in the Royal Armoury at Madrid. This weapon, which was originally in the armoury of the Emperor Charles V, though having a butt of German type, has a horn-veneered stock engraved with scrolling floral ornament in a Franco-Italian design while the butt is engraved *Vive Bourgogne* and dated 1537.

In spite of being subjected to German influence in the early stages of their development French wheellock weapons soon developed strong individual characteristics. While the locks produced in other countries have the entire mechanism mounted on the lockplate, the **French version** of the lock has the mainspring and wheel-arbor separate from the plate and fitted in the interior of the stock, which is hollowed out to receive them. The mainspring is retained in position by a stout steel pin which fits into the bend of the V-shaped spring. The wheel-arbor, which is connected to the mainspring by the usual short, linked chain as described earlier, has the end opposite to the key-square prolonged to pass through the side of the stock opposite the lock, where a hole drilled in the counterplate provides a bearing. It is therefore

Wheellock carbine of about 1570 made for the Duc de Montmorency. Length of barrel 27·9 in. Calibre ·50 in. 36 bore. Armouries, Tower of London.

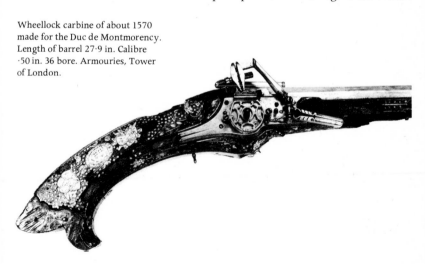

possible to remove the lock from the stock without disturbing the mainspring and wheel-arbor. There are two advantages in this design when compared with wheellocks of normal construction. The lock is lighter and can be made smaller, neater and more elegant in shape, while it is also more easily removed for cleaning, for it must be remembered that the users of wheellock and flint-lock guns removed the locks for cleaning every time they had been fired more than two or three times to remove the powder fouling which was apt to find its way into the interior of the lock through the joint between the edge of the pan and the barrel.

French wheellocks tend to have large wheels, and in order to accommodate them the lower edge of the lockplate is curved and follows the periphery of the wheel. The part of the stock below the lock is reinforced with a steel strap on which is mounted the trigger-guard, and in the front end there is a slot to accomodate

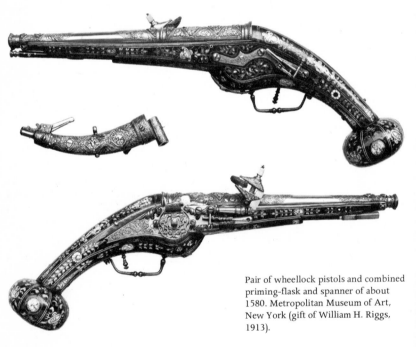

Pair of wheellock pistols and combined priming-flask and spanner of about 1580. Metropolitan Museum of Art, New York (gift of William H. Riggs, 1913).

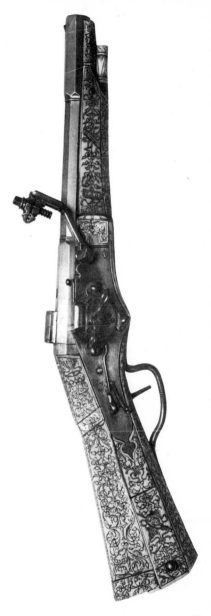

Wheellock pistol or carbine,
possibly French, dated 1537.
Real Armería, Madrid.

the end of the mainspring when unspanned, through which it is visible. This opening enables the chain connecting the end of the mainspring to be lubricated, which with chain, wheel-arbor and mainspring concealed inside the stock would otherwise be difficult, while removal of the strap makes it possible to extract the mainspring from the stock, should this be necessary. The lockplates are square at the front, while on early weapons the pointed rear end is finished with a notch. The **wheels on early examples** are kept in position by a bearing-plate covering the entire surface of the wheel and often pierced in a decorative design. On later specimens this form of bearing-plate was abandoned in favour of a quite small plate attached to the lockplate by a screw just behind the wheel and extending over only a small proportion of its surface. Although so small these plates fulfilled their purpose perfectly efficiently, this being to prevent the wheel being pushed outwards by the pressure of the sear and to keep it flat against the face of the lockplate. The change from one form of bearing-plate to the other occurred around 1600.

The French method of wheellock construction was perfectly practical and the locks functioned just as efficiently as those following the more massive German system. There was however one weakness in the design, namely that the hollowing out of the stock to accommodate the mainspring at the small of the butt, already its weakest point, weakened it still further and the stocks of French wheellock arms sometimes fractured, especially at the point where the pin securing the mainspring pierces the butt.

The shape of the French type of wheellock dictated the form of the stock, at least in the region of the lock, it being rounded to suit the contour of the lockplate. It has already been mentioned that the underside of the stock is covered by a steel strap to which the trigger-guard is attached, enabling the latter to be far more securely fixed than is the case with the trigger-guards of wheellock weapons made in other countries, which are merely screwed into the wood of the stock.

The earliest known firearm fitted with a wheellock of French type is a **short carbine** in the Royal Armoury, Madrid. This weapon, which may be dated around 1540, exhibits certain German characteristics such as a short club-like butt, stag-horn plaques inlaid in the stock, which however bear decoration engraved in a French style, a ring-shaped bearing-plate to the wheel and a German style of doghead, the latter unusually mounted behind the wheel instead of in front and having an internal spring. The lock however is already of French design, with the mainspring separate from the lockplate, the rear of which is notched in the manner characteristic of the earlier French locks. German fashion continued to influence French firearms as the 16th century advanced, but with national characteristics becoming more and more pronounced. Stocks continue to be decorated with stag-horn inlays and occasionally were even made with the large **flattened-ball butts** common to German pistols of the same period. The dogheads of the locks however begin to assume a baluster shape which is typically French around 1570, while the barrels lengthen as the century advances and at the same time are of smaller calibre. The barrels also develop a ridge or **shoulder** at the base of the breech which persists to around 1610, this being accompanied by a small **moulding** at the muzzle. About 1600 pistol butts become **ovoid in shape**, often with facetted or fluted sides.

More French wheellock pistols of the 16th century exist than guns, possibly due to the fact that pistols were always made in pairs, but those guns which have survived exhibit the same characteristics, the stocks usually having stag-horn decoration. The butts however soon show a marked difference from their German prototypes, and instead of retaining the short German form become longer and more slender.

Wheellock carbine, probably French, of about 1540–1550. Real Armería, Madrid.

15

Wheellock pistols of about 1600.
Left: length of barrel 24 in.
Calibre ·35 in. 95 bore. Right:
length of barrel 19 in. Calibre
·43 in. 60 bore. Armouries, Tower
of London.

The Early
17th Century

After 1600 German fashion ceased completely to influence French firearms. Bone or stag-horn inlay in stocks disappears, to be replaced by **scrollwork** inlaid in brass or silver wire with, occasionally, plaques of mother-of-pearl. The butts of guns, which survive from this later period in greater numbers, are now of shoulder length, albeit short by modern standards, and are of a moderate and graceful 'fishtail' form, the trigger-guards being long enough to be grasped by the middle, fourth and little fingers of the trigger hand. The lock, although retaining its basic form and method of construction, is now simplified. The **bearing-plates**, as noted above, are now reduced in size and only operate on the rear edge of the wheels while the pan-covers, which had previously often been closed by a press-stud release in the German fashion, are now often hand-operated. At the same time barrels, though still long and elegant, increase in calibre and the mouldings at breech and muzzle are abandoned. With these final refinements, which were introduced between 1595 and 1620, French wheellock firearms attained their fullest mechanical development while their graceful outlines and restrained ornament make them possibly the most attractive weapons of their type and period.

French wheellocks influenced the fashion in firearms beyond the borders of the country itself, notably in the Netherlands, Alsace and Lorraine (at this date not yet under French rule) and even southern Germany. In these regions however it was only

18, 19

19

Top view of wheellock pistol (16, right),
showing silver inlaid decoration.

the **external appearance of the locks** which was copied, the actual mechanism being of normal German type with the main-spring mounted on the inner side of the lockplate instead of being secured inside the stock.

As the 17th century advanced the French firearm industry increased in importance, this being at least partly due to royal patronage. Henry IV of France owned many firearms though probably only in the quantities which would be normal for a ruler of his time who enjoyed shooting; his son Louis XIII (1610–1642) on the other hand had a real love of guns and pistols and brought

19, 22 together a very considerable **collection** comprising, as well as those inherited from his father, large numbers acquired by himself, while it is known that as well as spending many hours shoot-

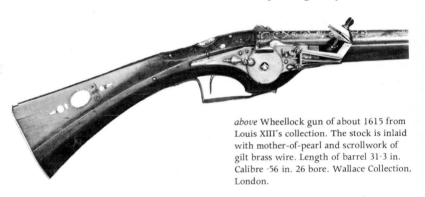

above Wheellock gun of about 1615 from Louis XIII's collection. The stock is inlaid with mother-of-pearl and scrollwork of gilt brass wire. Length of barrel 31·3 in. Calibre ·56 in. 26 bore. Wallace Collection, London.

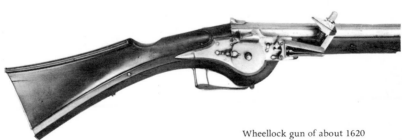

Wheellock gun of about 1620 from Louis XIII's collection. Length of barrel 39 in. Calibre ·66 in. 16 bore. Wallace Collection, London.

ing game and at target practice, the king took pleasure in stripping and cleaning his firearms with his own hands. Much is known about Louis XIII's arms collection since a list of the contents was drawn up in 1673 as part of an inventory of royal property made by order of Louis XIV. Each item was stamped with a number, usually on the underside of the stock, which corresponds with a short description in the inventory and from this those of the weapons which still exist can be identified.

The production of wheellocks in France must have been considerable in the last years of the lock's popularity, that is between 1620 and 1640, but the development of the flintlock was soon to make it obsolete. Before discussing the flintlock however a word must be said about the **snaphaunce**, a form of mechanism combining some of the features of both wheellock and flintlock. It resembles the flintlock in having a cock holding a flint striking forwards against a steel set in front of the pan, and resembles the wheellock in having a pan-cover separate from the steel and, at least in the earlier examples, a sear which penetrates the lockplate and engages with a recess in the cock. Weapons with snaphaunce locks appear to have been made in very small numbers in France. Certainly very few which can be definitely recognised as French have survived and it is probable that those which were produced followed the type made in Flanders.

Dutch wheellock pistols of about 1640–1650. Top: length of barrel 19·3 in. Calibre ·52 in. 32 bore. Bottom: length of barrel 13·9 in. Calibre ·53 in. 30 bore. Armouries, Tower of London.

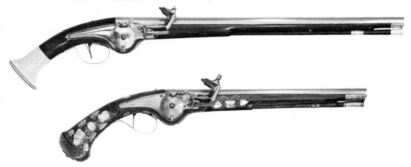

The Introduction of the Flintlock

The flintlock in the form in which it was to spread over the whole area of Western culture and remain in use for over two hundred years was almost certainly invented in France between 1610 and 1620 and can probably be attributed to one of two brothers, Marin and Jean le Bourgeois, gunmakers working at Lisieux in Normandy. Of the two earliest French flintlock guns in existence one, now in the Hermitage Museum, Leningrad, made either for Louis XIII or even possibly for Henri IV in the last year of his life (No. 152 in Louis XIII's collection) is signed by Marin le Bourgeois; the other, No. 134 in the king's *Cabinet d'Armes* and now in a private collection, bears a mark attributed to Jean le Bourgeois. The **flintlock** was certainly developed from the snaphaunce which it basically resembles but with the mechanism greatly simplified and improved. The cock was retained from the earlier lock together with the mainspring mounted on the front portion of the lockplate, but the steel was combined with the pan-cover which was therefore thrown back together with the steel by the blow of the flint. The combined steel and pan-cover was now known as the hammer, battery or, in more modern terminology, frizzen. The sear was pivoted vertically and engaged with two notches in the back of the tumbler, to which the cock was attached and on the toe of which the mainspring operated. When the cock was pulled back against the pressure of the mainspring the sear slipped first into the half-cock notch, in which position the cock was held vertically and away from the pan, then, when pulled

22, 63

still further back, into the full-cock notch. The notch for half-cock was so shaped that pressure on the trigger would not force the nose of the sear out of it and thus provided a safety position. The lock of a flintlock firearm was always set at half-cock while the weapon was being loaded or being carried while loaded.

22   The **cocks** of early flintlocks are long and slender and were prevented from falling so far forward that they could strike the pan by a stop or buffer secured by a screw to the outer face of the lockplate in front of the breast of the cock, this being a feature retained from the snaphaunce. From about 1630 however the cocks began to be made with a ledge or shoulder on the inner side of the base of the neck which engaged with the upper edge of the lockplate and made the buffer unnecessary. On early flintlocks

22, 24   the **spring** for the frizzen was mounted on the inner side of the lockplate and was not fitted externally until about 1640, when it assumed the position it was to retain, with only occasional exceptions, to the end of the flintlock era. In France flintlocks seem to have been fitted at first mainly to guns rather than to pistols,

Flintlock gun of about 1620–1630 from Louis XIII's collection. Length of barrel 54·5 in. Calibre ·70 in. 13 bore. Armouries, Tower of London.

One of a pair of flintlock pistols by
Le Conte, Paris. Length of barrel
17·7 in. Calibre ·53 in. 30 bore.
Wallace Collection, London.

which continued to be produced with wheellock mechanisms,
this probably being due to the obvious advantages of the flintlock
for sporting purposes. The custom of shooting game on the wing
was becoming fashionable early in the 17th century and may have
been connected with the introduction of flintlock fowling-pieces,
the lightness and better balance of the flintlock gun and the
greater safety provided by the half-cock position on the lock all
being in its favour when flying shots became the order of the day.
Possibly because of the new fashion in shooting the stocks even
of quite early flintlock guns are longer and more solid than those
of their wheellock predecessors and the guns were a comfortable
fit when brought up to the shoulder.

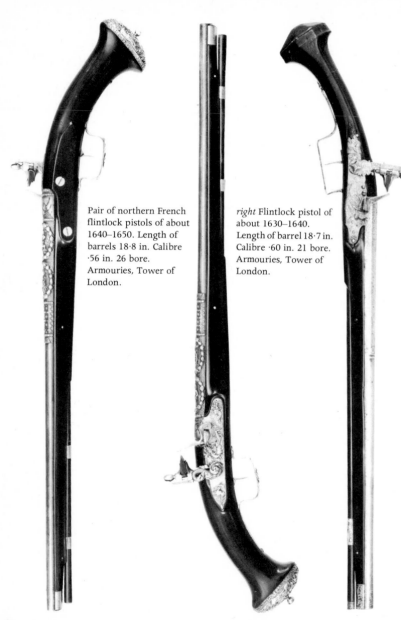

Pair of northern French flintlock pistols of about 1640–1650. Length of barrels 18·8 in. Calibre ·56 in. 26 bore. Armouries, Tower of London.

right Flintlock pistol of about 1630–1640. Length of barrel 18·7 in. Calibre ·60 in. 21 bore. Armouries, Tower of London.

Decoration was still restrained, consisting on the finer weapons, both guns and pistols, of silver inlays in the stocks while the locks were engraved or etched with foliage or scrollwork. Barrels were blued and the breech section damascened with scrollwork in gold, which makes a most attractive effect against the blue background. By the 1640s the barrels themselves are externally of octagonal section at the breech, this section continuing for about a third of their length, after which they are of round section to the muzzle, the change of section, after 1640, being effected by the **facets** becoming sixteen-sided for a short distance and gradually merging into the round forward portion—a very simple but graceful device. From this date also it became usual for the gunmaker to place his name on the barrel, usually inlaid in gold on expensive pieces to harmonise with the gold decoration at the breech. When this fashion was established the maker's marks which in the 16th and early 17th century had often been stamped on the upper surface of the breech were placed instead on the underside in order not to spoil the scheme of decoration. The maker's name is also frequently engraved on the lockplate, often accompanied by the name of the town where he worked.

By the mid 1630s pistols fitted with flintlocks began to be produced. These were almost invariably **long-barrelled holster pistols** of the same proportions as the wheellock weapons they soon superseded. The flintlocks with which they are fitted differ in no way from those of the guns already described although the spring controlling the frizzen is fitted on the inner side of the lockplate more frequently than is the case with the fowling-pieces, the reason probably being that this method of construction gave a smoother surface to the lock which was therefore less likely to catch when the pistol was being placed in its holster. It should perhaps be explained that these long pistols were intended as weapons for a mounted man and were carried in a pair of leather holsters attached to a metal D on either side of the saddlebow, the ends of the holsters being secured by loops to the breast-strap of the harness. The stocks of the pistols, apart from losing the rounded bulge on the underside which had been necessitated by the shape of the wheellock, had from the beginning a different shape

25

of butt, the oviform butts of the wheellock pistols being replaced by a flattened **fishtail shape** usually finished with a slightly convex metal cap, this form of butt also being sometimes found on very late wheellock examples. In the period around 1640 butts of silver or bronze gilt were also found, cast and chased in the shape of human, animal or birds' heads, and doubtless looking very fine projecting from the open tops of saddle-holsters.

23, 24

The long slender cocks of the early French flintlocks were delicate and liable to breakage and by 1645 the design was altered, the cock becoming shorter. As an extra insurance against damage the lower jaw was connected with the breast of the cock by a **convex scroll** forming an almost circular aperture. This type of cock, often known in modern parlance as a 'ring-necked' cock, was to persist until late in the century when it was abandoned, to be revived a hundred years later for military locks. Sometimes the concave curve at the back of the lock was treated in the same

23, 35

Flintlock gun made about 1675 by Gruché, Paris. Armouries, Tower of London.

manner and both connecting scrolls were in many cases decoratively treated.

Locks were still made with flat surfaces up to 1660, but around this date the lockplate and cock began to develop a rounded form on their outer face. This new fashion first affected the cock, then the rear of the lockplate, and finally by 1670 the **whole lockplate** was treated in this manner. As well as the alteration in external form the 1660s saw the introduction of a small but important refinement to the lock mechanism. This was the addition of a bearing-plate or bridle to provide additional support to the sear. This bearing-plate gave a smoother action to the lock mechanism and reduced the wear which took place at the point where the tumbler bore upon its opening in the lockplate.

In this same period (1660–1670) the stocks of both guns and pistols underwent a change of shape. The **butts of guns** lost the convex curve on the underside and were made with a straight line

26, 27

28

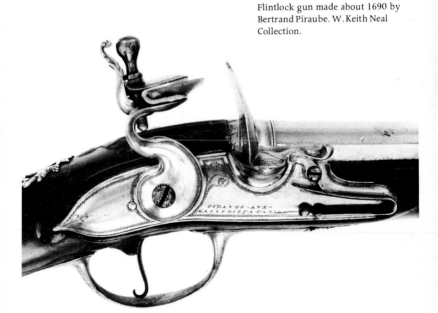

Flintlock gun made about 1690 by Bertrand Piraube. W. Keith Neal Collection.

to the lower edge, assuming in fact the form which the butts of all firearms intended to be discharged from the shoulder have retained to the present day. As regards pistols, the fishtail butts now began to have a more rounded profile while the butt-caps became larger and more deeply convex and developed short projections in the centre on either side reaching forward along the wood of the butt. From this period also derives the development of the screw-plate, counter-plate or side-plate, as it is variously called. The lock was secured in position by two screws which passed from left to right through passages drilled in the stock. In order to prevent the heads of the screws biting into the wood when screwed home it became usual by 1650 to fit a simple metal plate, usually S-shaped, to the left side of the stock, the ends of which corresponded with the screw passages and therefore formed a protective surface for the wood. The decorative potential of the screw-plates was soon realised by the makers of mounts for firearms and by the 1660s the plates were no longer simple and flush-fitting but were made to stand proud of the wood of the stock and began to develop decorative **scrolled appendages** which became more and more elaborate as the century advanced.

From 1670 French firearms of fine quality became more richly ornamented. The taste of the age of Louis XIV tended towards grandeur and outward display. The king himself set the fashion and the French nobility and gentry who crowded to the court at the newly built Chateau of Versailles spent vast sums on their

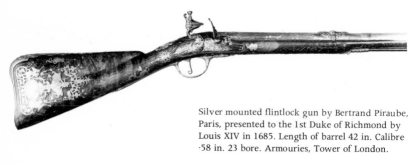

Silver mounted flintlock gun by Bertrand Piraube, Paris, presented to the 1st Duke of Richmond by Louis XIV in 1685. Length of barrel 42 in. Calibre ·58 in. 23 bore. Armouries, Tower of London.

Side- or screw-plate of gun (27).

Side- or screw-plate of gun (left).

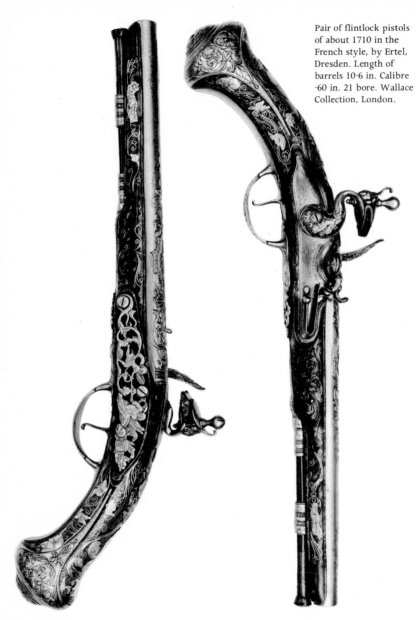

Pair of flintlock pistols of about 1710 in the French style, by Ertel, Dresden. Length of barrels 10·6 in. Calibre ·60 in. 21 bore. Wallace Collection, London.

houses, furniture, wearing apparel and in fact everything connected with day-to-day life. Louis actively encouraged this for he liked his courtiers to make a brave show, since it served to impress foreign visitors with the power and wealth of France. This tendency towards increased outward display was reflected in firearms made for private ownership and from 1670 more elaborate decoration was employed. In addition to the beautiful blued barrels with their gold damascening the mounts, now more massive than formerly, began to be chiselled and chased with **designs in relief** and were quite often made of **silver** as well as of steel, while the walnut stocks were frequently enriched with carving, though this was never carried to excess and was usually confined to the area surrounding the breech-strap of the barrel and the ramrod throat-pipe. The **stocks** of some firearms of exceptionally fine quality were lavishly inlaid with decoration in silver as well as being silver mounted.

Louis XIV himself was not a lover of firearms for their own sake, as his father had been, but he was still passionately fond of both hunting and shooting and was an excellent shot, it being recorded that in 1714, when he was already suffering from the maladies which were to cause his death a year later, he killed thirty-two pheasants with thirty-four shots, a score which a sportsman of the present day using a hammerless ejector gun would be proud of achieving. The king's love of shooting is demonstrated by the **fine paintings** by Desportes of his favourite sporting dogs, mostly painted for his favourite week-end retreat, the Chateau de Marly, and now to be seen in the Musée de la Chasse in Paris.

A typical sporting gun of this period had a barrel about fifty inches long with a calibre of around ·60 of an inch, or 20 bore, and weighed about 7 lb. Pistols were shorter than in the early years of the century with barrels around twelve to fourteen inches long and usually about 20 bore. In the second half of the 17th century French firearm design had considerable influence on firearms produced in other countries, not only as regards their lock construction but also as regards their decoration. This influence was catered to by the production of **engraved patterns** specifically intended to be of use to the gunmakers. These pattern books,

Bonne, Nonne and Ponne, three of Louis XIV's sporting dogs, painted by François Desportes in about 1700. Musée de la Chasse et de la Nature, Paris.

which had been initiated by Phillipe Cordier Daubigny in the 1630s, were produced by several different artists at various dates in the course of the 17th and 18th centuries and found a ready sale outside the borders of France itself. Another factor which led to the spread of French design was the Revocation of the Edict of Nantes in 1685. Several of the most skilful French gunmakers were Huguenots and these, driven abroad to Holland, Germany, England and other Protestant countries, settled in their land of adoption and continued making weapons in the French style. In some countries, **notably Germany**, these weapons influenced the native gunmakers, though it is also a fact that in most of the countries of Europe the French style in general was in any case in fashion.

Design for the decoration of gunlocks from *Livre de diverses ordonnances* by Thomas Picquot, Paris, 1638.

opposite Designs for the decoration of firearms from *Plusieurs Models . . . qui sont en usages en l'Art de Arquebuserie*, published by the gunmakers Thuraine and Le Hollandois in 1660.

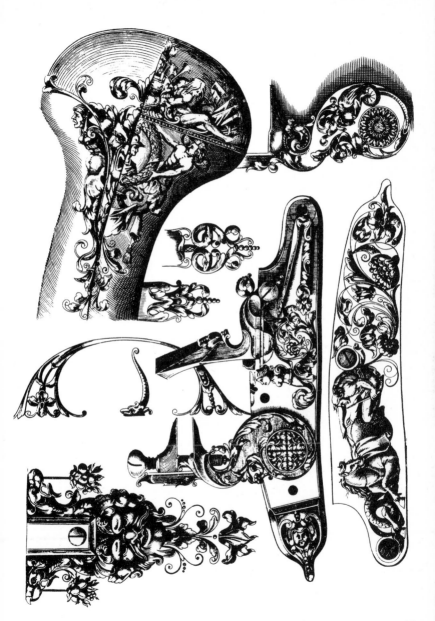

The 18th Century

Almost exactly at the year 1700 there was a marked change in the form of the French flintlock; the convex rounded forms in vogue since the 1660s giving way to **flat surfaces** which are reminiscent of the fashion of sixty years earlier. With the new fashion the outlines of the lock remained the same but the lockplate and cock were flat with bevelled edges, while the back of the steel and the underside of the pan were facetted to match. There was also a tendency to reduce the rear section of the lockplate in depth in relation to the main forward portion, thus easing the merging of the rear of the lock into the grip of the stock. In this period the octagonal breech end of the barrels no longer evolved into the round front part by means of a series of facets but merged gradually, with the exception of the **top flat** which was continued as a sighting rib as far as the foresight. Stocks of both guns and pistols became slimmer and more elegant, the mounts often being a combination of steel and silver, the trigger-guard, heel-plate or butt-cap and ramrod pipes being of steel for greater strength, while the counter-plate and escutcheon plate on the small of the butt were of silver. The projections on the sides of the pistol butt-caps, which had appeared in the 1660s, had developed by the 1670s into long slender **extensions** reaching nearly as far as the locks and served to strengthen the butt at the point where it was narrowed to form a grip for the hand. By 1700 steel butt-caps were often set with a **silver medallion** in the centre, in the form of a lion's mask or classical head. Chiselled decoration was less used

Lock of holster pistol of about 1730.
Author's Collection.

Inner side of above lock, showing
mechanism.

on locks and mounts after 1700 and only occurs on very grand
38 weapons, when it is set against a **gold ground**, producing a very
rich effect. Most of the new flat lockplates however were merely
engraved with a classical figure or two and a trophy.

There was little change in form between 1700 and the middle
years of the 18th century, the only one of importance being in the
39 design of the **counter-plate** which in about 1740 usually ceased
to be pierced and chased in a decorative design and became flat
and similar in size and general shape to the lockplate, which it
balanced on the opposite side.

40 **Small pistols** of pocket size seem to have been little produced
in France before the 18th century, or if they were few have survived, but in the period under discussion they became more
common and were often attractive little weapons, scaled-down
versions of their larger brothers the holster pistols.

The next change in style took place around 1760. As far as the
locks were concerned this consisted in a reversion to the **rounded**
41, 43 **forms** in fashion eighty years earlier, the flat lockplates and cocks
with bevelled edges being abandoned and convex surfaces taking
their place. A mechanical refinement introduced contemporane-
ously with the change in the lock consisted of a bridle joining the
screw on which the frizzen hinged to the front edge of the pan.
By this means this particular screw, which is the one of the whole
lock subjected to the greatest mechanical strain, was given support at two points instead of at one. After the introduction of this
bridle the frizzen screw was put in from the back of the lockplate

Flintlock pistol with chiselled decoration, made
about 1720 by Chasteau, Paris. Length of barrel
14 in. Calibre ·62 in. 21 bore. Wallace Collection,
London.

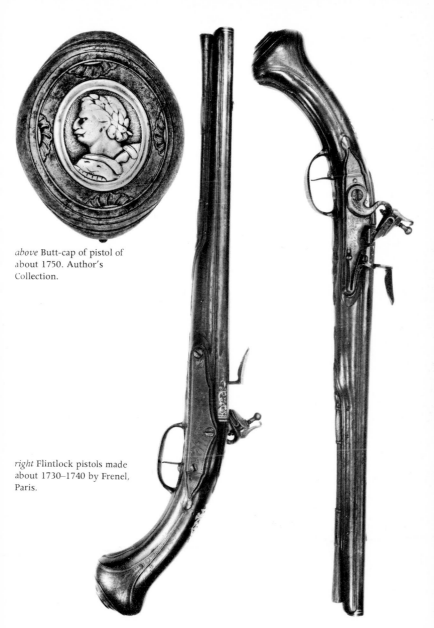

above Butt-cap of pistol of about 1750. Author's Collection.

right Flintlock pistols made about 1730–1740 by Frenel, Paris.

instead of the front, giving the lock a neater appearance. Pistol stocks altered little in this period of changing style, although the
42 butts were given a slightly **sharper downward curve** while the barrels, even of holster pistols, became rather shorter. Gun-butts however begin to show a slight concave shape on the underside when viewed in profile, while the small of the butt or grip is longer, resulting in the butt itself being shorter and having a less
43 graceful shape than before. A **pad** covered with leather or velvet was often placed on the left side of the butt to prevent the user's right cheek being bruised by the recoil of the gun, this being a peculiarly French fashion only rarely met with in other countries. Trigger-guard bows of both guns and pistols became larger and

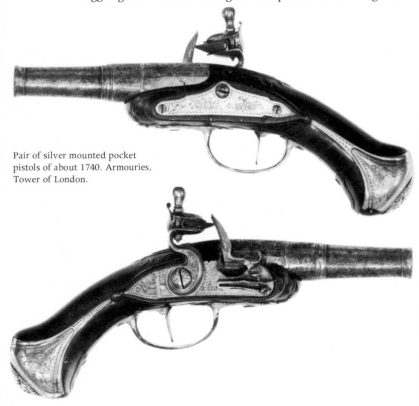

Pair of silver mounted pocket pistols of about 1740. Armouries, Tower of London.

wider, narrowing abruptly to a slender front pillar and divided at the rear. With guns, the rear finial plate was swept outwards from the wood of the stock, which it rejoined at the end in a curl, thus forming what is known as a **scroll-shaped guard**, the object being to lessen the bend of the wrist of the right hand when grasping the small of the butt. This fashion was also adopted in England in the 1770s though the curl given to the finial was more pronounced. The manner of fastening the barrel to the stock was also improved. Until now the barrel had been secured at the breech end by a long screw which pierced the breech-strap and screwed into the trigger-plate, while the forward end of the barrel was fastened by slender pins which were driven transversely through

43

Lock of a double-barrelled gun of about 1785, an early work of Nicholas Boutet. Armouries, Tower of London.

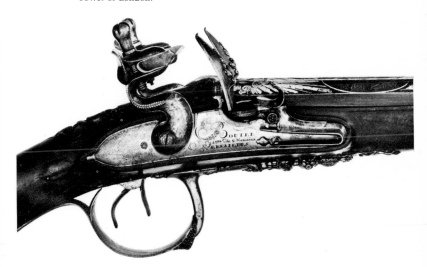

the fore-end, passing through narrow loops in the underside of the barrel. A device known as a false-breech was now introduced, possibly from England where it was already in fashion, consisting of a solid steel block screwed to the stock in the same manner as the breech-strap of the barrel had been and having a rectangular aperture on its face, while the breech end of the barrel was made with a blunt hook which was inserted into the aperture; the **pins** securing the barrel to the fore-end were made wide and flat with one flattened end which prevented them being driven too far into the wood. This improvement made it far easier to remove the barrel from the stock, an important factor when the barrel was being washed out to remove the powder fouling left in the bore after a day's shooting.

42, 43

Pair of double-barrelled flintlock pistols made about 1770 by Lallemand, Tours. Length of barrels 9·9 in. Calibre ·54 in. 29 bore. Armouries, Tower of London.

Flintlock gun by Soupriant, Paris, bearing the arms of the Comte d'Artois. Silver mounts hallmarked for 1776. Length of barrel 38·2 in. Calibre ·62 in. 19 bore. Wallace Collection, London.

From the early days of gunmaking barrels had been made by bending a flat strip of iron round a mandrel under heat until the edges met and formed a tube, and then hammer-welding them together. In France it became usual after 1750 for a barrel-smith, when producing a good quality barrel, to strengthen it by winding a narrow ribbon of iron spirally around the original tube, the ribbon being continually heated and the edges again hammer-welded together. The barrel was then bored out so as to leave only a thin sleeve of the iron tube between it and the spirally wound ribbon. Weapons fitted with these superior barrels often advertise the fact by having the words *Canon Tordu* (twisted barrel) or *Canon à Ruban* (ribbon barrel) inlaid in gold on their upper surface.

41 **Double-barrelled** sporting guns now began for the first time to be made in some numbers. A few had been produced in the earlier years of the century but the barrels had simply been fastened in the stock side by side, no attempt being made to join them other than by the bands securing them to the fore-end. Due to the improvements effected in the manufacture of gunpowder by the middle of the century barrels could now be made shorter than previously and gunmakers found it possible to join two barrels side by side by soldering them to each other and to a rib, a strip of steel which ran their full length on the upper surface and also formed a sighting channel, carrying the foresight at the muzzle end.

From Flintlock
to Percussion

The French Revolution brought to an end for a time the production of fine quality weapons in France as it did the production of most articles not of a military nature. The moneyed clients of the old régime were no more, while the new wealthy classes of the Consulate and Empire with their fortunes made from army contracts had to yet appear. The first sporting weapons of more than average quality to be made after the turmoil of the 1790s was over were produced for the Government and were the products of a single maker. Nicholas Noel Boutet had been a gunmaker to the king, *Arquebusier du Roi*, before the Revolution but nevertheless was in 1792 made director of the new government arms manufactory established in the building known as the Grand Commun which housed the administration of the Château of Versailles. From 1794 there began to be produced in these workshops not only the military weapons for which they had been established but also weapons, many of the first quality, which were given as presents by the government to distinguished officers and government officials and also to foreign royalty. Swords as well as firearms were produced at Versailles but it is only the latter that need concern us. The guns and pistols made at the *Manufacture de Versailles* differed markedly in their decoration from any made in the 18th century. The Rococo scrollwork chiselled on the locks and mounts of the finer weapons of the earlier period now gave way to ornament based on classical models though the effect was no less rich than before. Barrels and locks were damascened in gold, so thickly inlaid that it could be worked with a tool to render the detail, this taking the form of classical vases, attenuated pyramids, flaming braziers and acanthus foliage, the locks, as an alternative, sometimes having sporting scenes. Gun butts were of similar form to those in vogue in the last years of the previous century but the scroll trigger-guard was abandoned, the same effect as regards the grip afforded to the right hand being achieved by increasing the depth of the stock at the same point, the wood then being **carved** to form an animal's head or a grotesque mask, the carving on the best guns being of excellent quality.

45

For a really important gift the Versailles manufactory produced two guns, a pair of pistols and a rifle or carbine. Few rifles had been made in France until this date due to the fact that it was the French fashion to hunt the stag mounted and with hounds rather than with a firearm but now, though the mounted stag-hunt remained in fashion with those rich enough to afford the accompanying outlay, many sportsmen with less long purses shot deer with the rifle as had been done in Germany and, to a lesser extent, England, for many years past. The new **rifles** had octagonal barrels with polygrooved or 'hair' rifling, sometimes consisting of over a hundred fine grooves, many of the barrels being ornamented with small gold stars, producing a most attractive effect.

46

Flintlock gun by Boutet et Fils, made about 1815 when Boutet's son had been taken into partnership. Length of barrel 38·3 in. Calibre ·66 in. $16\frac{1}{2}$ bore. Wallace Collection, London.

Flintlock rifle produced about 1805 in Nicholas Boutet's workshops at the *Manufacture de Versailles*. Length of barrel 25·7 in. Calibre ·60 in. 21 bore. Wallace Collection, London.

The pistols produced in the Versailles workshops were markedly different from those of the 18th century. The **butts** were curved sharply downwards so that the barrel formed almost a right angle to the hand of the firer, the ends of the butts being finished flat with a shallow butt-cap which no longer had extensions projecting up the sides of the grip as previously. The butt-caps were often formed as a mask in cast and chased silver. Pistol barrels were similar to those of the rifles in being octagonal in form and having hair rifling. They also frequently carried the same decoration of gold stars. The stocks of Boutet's finest presentation firearms were frequently inlaid with **decoration in gold**, usually cut out of thin sheet on which detail could be engraved.

These richly decorated weapons had certain mechanical refinements. An **anti-friction roller** was introduced between the heel of the frizzen and its spring while the internal mechanism of

48

46, 48

45, 46, 48

the lock was also given a smoother action by means of a hinged link connecting the mainspring to the tumbler. Both these improvements may have been due to English influence like the false-breech barrel-fastening already noted, for English influence on French culture was considerable in the late 18th and early 19th centuries in spite of the frequent state of war between the two countries.

As the Consulate gave place to the Empire and wealthy clients increased in number other gunmakers joined Boutet as producers of fine firearms, such as Le Page, Napoleon's personal gunmaker, Armand and Pirmet. Napoleon is known to have been a poor shot though the story that it was he who was responsible for Marshal Massena being blinded in one eye through being hit by a shot pellet during an imperial shooting party at Fontainebleau is apocryphal, the culprit in fact being Marshal Berthier.

Early in the 1800s it became usual for fine pistols to be sold fitted into wooden boxes or cases sometimes covered in leather. These were usually velvet-lined and the interiors were partitioned so that each pistol of the pair lay snugly in its own compartment, with separate compartments for the tools and other accessories for cleaning and loading such as a bullet-mould, powder-flask and screwdriver. The sporting rifles produced by Boutet 50, 51 and his contemporaries were also often sold in **cases**.

The design of French firearms altered little between 1800 and the end of the flintlock era in 1820. It was not uncommon by 1810 for the trigger-guards of pistols to be fitted with a spur, a short member curving forwards from the rear of the bow around which the second finger could be curled, giving a firmer and more rigid grip. This refinement was especially favoured by those who used their pistols for duelling, for the pistol duel as a method of settling private quarrels was now fashionable, although the sword duel was never entirely abandoned in France.

The flintlock, perfected in France in the early years of the 17th century, had had a long life-span but by the second decade of the 19th century its days were numbered. It had long been known that when certain metals were dissolved in acid, salts were formed which would explode with great violence when struck a blow

Pair of flintlock pistols made about 1810 in Boutet's
workshops at Versailles. Length of barrels 10·4 in.
Calibre ·66 in. 16 bore. Wallace Collection, London.

with a hard implement. The principle was known in the 17th century and Pepys refers to it in his diary (11th November 1663).

Experiments continued to be made in the following century, notably, in France, by Berthollet who experimented successfully with fulminate of silver in 1788, but all the early experimenters were at fault in believing that fulminating compounds could be used as a substitute for gunpowder, or could be mixed with gunpowder, which was in fact impractical since the explosion of fulminate is too violent and uncontrollable for the substances to be employed in large quantities. The answer to the problem of the uses of fulminates in firearms was finally found in or about the year 1805 by a Scottish clergyman, the Reverend Alexander Forsyth, Rector of Belhelvie in Aberdeenshire. Forsyth realised that the way to employ fulminate successfully in a firearm was not as a main charge but as a means of ignition, and designed a lock using fulminate of mercury which he patented in 1807. Forsyth's fulminant or, to give it the name by which it was usually known, detonator lock, used the fulminating compound in the form of powder, but this could easily be compacted into a solid and produced in the form of small cakes or wafers. Who it was who first placed a wafer of fulminating compound in the base of a little metal tube closed at one end and open at the other, then placed it on a hollow steel peg or nipple communicating with the powder chamber of the barrel and exploded it by the descent of the cock, is not definitely known. The chief claimants to the invention of the percussion-cap are Joshua Shaw, an American painter, who claimed to have invented it in 1814 but who did not in fact take out a patent until 1822; Colonel Peter Hawker, the famous expert on shooting, who stated that he suggested the idea to the London Gunmaker Joseph Manton; and Prelat, a Parisian gunmaker who included a primitive form of cap in a patent covering several forms of fulminate ignition in 1818, while the first patent devoted solely to a percussion-cap and nipple lies to the credit of Deboubert, another French gunmaker, this being taken out in France in 1820. These various claims will probably never be resolved, but the facts are that by 1822 percussion ignition was established and five years later, in France as in England, sporting guns fitted with flintlocks were only being made for a very few ultra-conservative sportsmen or for those whose travels took them to far-off places where copper caps were difficult to obtain. The new ignition system was an obvious improvement on the flintlock. The flame from the explosion of the copper percussion-cap was directed into the powder charge through a passage enclosed for its whole length, whereas in the flintlock the powder was ignited by sparks falling into a priming-pan, the flame from which then had to pass through the touch-hole passage. The new system was far less susceptible to damp, while guns fitted with the new system shot more strongly than their predecessors since with the flintlock a certain proportion

Double-barrelled rifle made about 1805 by Boutet, Versailles, in its velvet-lined leather case. Length of barrels 23·5 in. Calibre ·50 in. 37 bore. Wallace Collection, London.

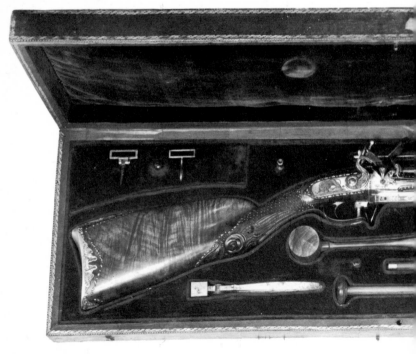

Case of rifle (below).

Cased pair of percussion duelling pistols made about
1825 by Lepage, Paris.

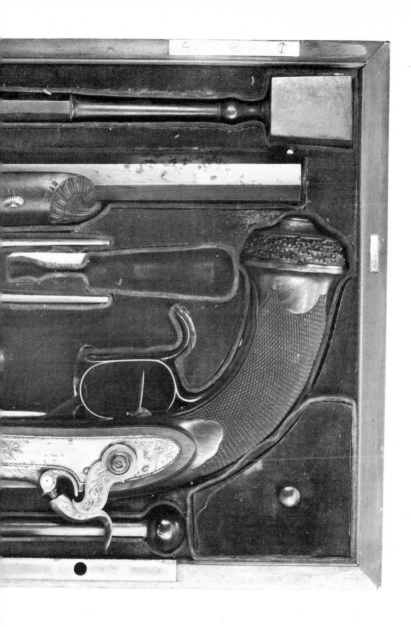

of the force of the discharge had inevitably escaped through the touch-hole.

Apart from the simplified appearance of the lock itself percussion guns showed little change of form compared to the flint-lock weapons made a few years previously. Most sporting guns of good quality were now double-barrelled and French guns continued to be characterised by carving on the grip at the small of the butt. French pistols however changed in style between the 1820s and 1840s. Weapons of the **early percussion period** followed the fashion established twenty years earlier in having sharply down-curved butts and octagonal barrels of fairly large bore with fine polygroove rifling. In the mid 1830s however there was a marked change. **Butts** became wider, flatter and had far less curve, allowing the pistol in fact to sit more comfortably in the hand, while the wood was carved with parallel mouldings and fluting which both gave a decorative effect and afforded a good grip to the hand. Barrels were of reduced calibre and while still sometimes octagonal were frequently made octagonal only at the breech and for a short distance at the muzzle, fluted in between. The bore was now rarely more than 0·5 of an inch and the earlier fine polygroove rifling was abandoned in favour of the more conventional type with six to nine lands and quite wide grooves between them. The fore-end was shortened and only extended about six inches in front of the trigger-guard, the front eight inches or so of the barrel being entirely exposed and unprotected. With the new short fore-end the ramrod was no longer carried in the stock beneath the barrel and a separate loading-rod was used which fitted into the case with which the pistols were invariably provided. These loading-rods were sometimes made of wood but were also often of brass or steel since the ball, wrapped in a thin greased linen patch, fitted tightly in the bore and had to be driven down the barrel with considerable force. To this end most French pistol cases of this period include among the accessories a **mallet** which was used in conjunction with the loading-rod to drive the ball down the rifled barrel and seat it firmly on top of the powder charge. The trigger-guard almost invariably had a **spur** for the second finger such as had been introduced in the late flintlock period. The pistols described above were intended for duelling and target practice and from the comparatively large numbers which have survived must have been produced in fair quantities. One of the best known makers was Gastinne Renette whose premises near the Rond Point des Champs Elysées housed a shooting gallery in the basement where men in fashionable society would spend a few hours now and then at pistol practice.

One of a pair of percussion duelling pistols, dated 1839, by Gastinne Renette, Paris. Length of barrel 10·7 in. Calibre ·50 in. 36 bore. Author's Collection.

Early Cartridge Breech-loaders

Muzzle-loading percussion weapons had a very short life compared with their flintlock forerunners. Coming into general use in the early 1820s, they were already being superseded twenty-five years later.

To trace the history of the breech-loading cartridge gun in France it is necessary to return briefly to the early years of the 19th century. Attempts to design a satisfactory breech-loader are almost as old as the history of hand-firearms. Many designs had been produced, some in France, several being of an ingenious and apparently not impractical nature, but all had failed on two main points; the early breech-loaders leaked gas at the breech, while the mechanisms, even if of quite simple design, became unworkable after only a few shots due to the residue left by the black powder then in use. The breech system which provided at least an almost complete answer to these two problems was the invention of Samuel Johannes Pauly, a Swiss who took up residence in France and in 1812 patented a specification for a breech-loading firearm which overcame the difficulties encountered by former designers. **Pauly's guns** had a breech-block which was hinged to the base of the barrel and lifted upwards for the insertion of the cartridge. The firing-pin was fitted in the breech block, the striker in a substantial metal frame below. The striker had to be drawn back manually by means of an external cocking lever but this gun was in effect a hammerless design. Pauly also included pistols in his patent specification,

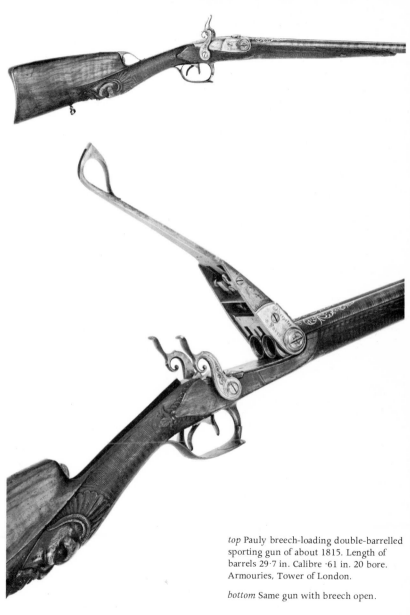

top Pauly breech-loading double-barrelled sporting gun of about 1815. Length of barrels 29·7 in. Calibre ·61 in. 20 bore. Armouries, Tower of London.

bottom Same gun with breech open.

57

these having a barrel which dropped downwards for loading. The design of breech and firing mechanism was ingenious but the most important part of the invention lay in the cartridge. This consisted of a short **base**, usually of brass, to which was fastened a tube of paper containing the charge. The patent specification refers to the paper tube being tied or glued to the base but cartridge bases which have survived are usually provided with a threaded projection on the inner side which was screwed into a card wad to which the paper cylinder was fastened by glue. The metal base had a circular depression in the centre of the outer face into which was pressed a cake or pill of fulminating compound, a small passage drilled in the centre of the depression taking the flash to the powder charge. The metal bases were made with a projecting rim which married with a rebate or groove cut in the end of the barrel, all in the manner of a modern shotgun.

Though the Pauly breech may have leaked a certain amount of gas on discharge the leak must have been small compared to that of any previous design and was not serious enough to interfere with its operation. With his pattern of breech and accompanying cartridge Pauly had in fact produced a hammerless centre-fire breech-loader. The gun was tested by competent authorities who reported favourably on it and quite a number

58

Brass bases for Pauly cartridges.

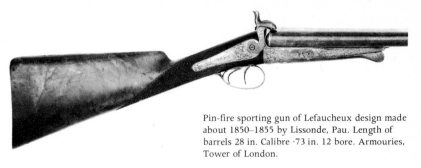

Pin-fire sporting gun of Lefaucheux design made about 1850–1855 by Lissonde, Pau. Length of barrels 28 in. Calibre ·73 in. 12 bore. Armouries, Tower of London.

were produced, the sportsmen who bought them apparently expressing every satisfaction. The Pauly system however suffered from the fate attending many other inventions, that of being before its time. The mechanism was delicate and needed to be made with great precision, surviving specimens of Pauly guns being in fact of first class workmanship. It was not considered suitable for military use; the army rejected it and on the fall of the Empire in 1814 Pauly made his way to England where he spent the last years of his life unprofitably in designing and attempting to construct an airship in partnership with his Swiss compatriot, the London gunmaker Durs Egg.

On Pauly's departure for England his business in Paris at 4 rue des Trois Frères was continued by the gunmaker Prelat, mentioned earlier, who had been in partnership with him and who continued for a few years to produce guns of Pauly design which still bore the inventor's name. Finally, in 1826, the business was taken over by Casimir Lefaucheux. The period between 1830 and 1860 is one of many inventions in the field of firearms. Pauly had shown that a breech-loader employing a cartridge with self-contained ignition was a practical proposition and it was only a matter of time before further improvements were made.

In 1832 Lefaucheux patented a breech-loading gun which may be considered as the direct ancestor of the sporting guns
59, 60   in general use today. The **Lefaucheux gun** had barrels which dropped downwards on a hinge for loading in the manner of a modern gun, the breech being opened, and secured when closed,

by a pivoted lever which lay along the underside of the fore-end. Operation of this rotated a flanged block which locked into a T-shaped slot in a lump on the underside of the barrel.

The cartridge had a brass or copper base attached to a case made of combustible paper, and was ignited by a percussion-cap placed on a nipple on top of the barrel in the manner of a muzzle-loader. In 1835 however, Lefaucheux amended his earlier patent to cover a new cartridge for use in a gun of his 1832 design. This **cartridge** had a brass base with a case of stiff paper; a percussion-cap was positioned in the base and opposite to it was a short brass rod or pin which projected beyond the rim of the base. When the cartridge was inserted into the chamber of

above Lefaucheux gun (59) with breech open.
Pin-fire sporting gun cartridges.

the barrel the pin projected through a slot fashioned in the upper rear edge of the latter and was driven downwards into the percussion-cap by the blow of the external hammer, thus discharging the cartridge. This system, known in England as pin-fire, provided a completely practical, reliable weapon. The paper case of the cartridge, soon improved by being made from card, was expanded against the walls of the chamber by the explosion and constituted an efficient gas seal. The gun was simple and practical; it could be easily loaded and unloaded and if a spent case jammed in the breech it could be extracted with a special tool which the sportsman carried in his pocket or suspended round his neck on a cord.

In 1845 Eugène Lefaucheux, son of Casimir, adapted his father's invention for a revolver and this and the guns were shown at the Great Exhibition in London in 1851, after which the pin-fire system was rapidly taken up by the English gunmakers, who soon produced their own versions though improving the method of locking the breech.

The year of 1850 is in some ways a watershed in the history of fine quality French firearms. Weapons produced in France had been among the finest ever made and in the 17th century had led the world in decoration and mechanical design, but in the second half of the 19th century there was a decline, perhaps initiated or accelerated by the fall of the Second Empire. In the latter half of the 19th century it became quite usual to import barrels and sometimes complete weapons from Liège, the great centre of the Belgian firearms industry, while wealthy sportsmen often preferred to buy their guns in England rather than from native makers.

> As brevity is my intention
> I purposely omit to mention
> Many more matters which you'll find
> In shooting books, if you're inclin'd.

W. Watt, *Remarks on Shooting*, London, 1835.

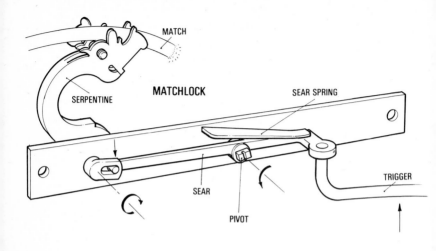

MATCH

MATCHLOCK

SERPENTINE

SEAR SPRING

TRIGGER

SEAR

PIVOT

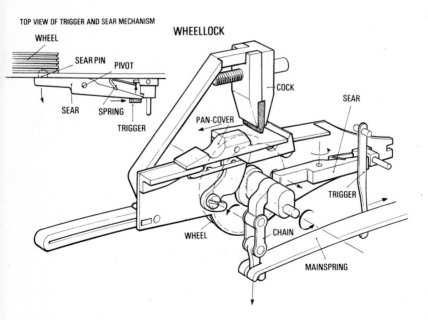

TOP VIEW OF TRIGGER AND SEAR MECHANISM

WHEELLOCK

WHEEL

SEAR PIN   PIVOT

COCK

SEAR

SEAR   SPRING

PAN-COVER

TRIGGER

TRIGGER

WHEEL   CHAIN

MAINSPRING

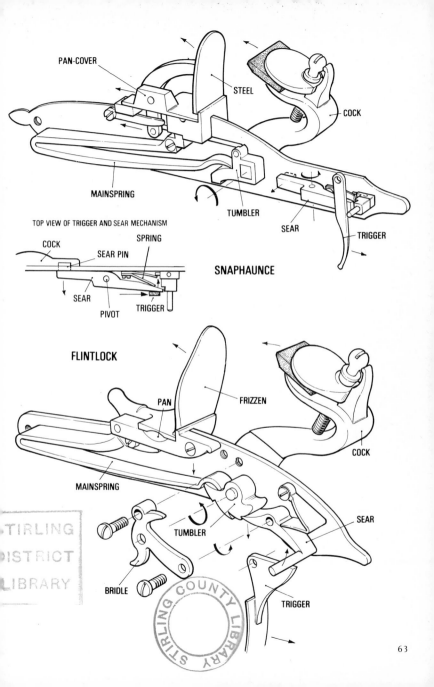

PAN-COVER

STEEL

COCK

MAINSPRING

TUMBLER

SEAR

TRIGGER

TOP VIEW OF TRIGGER AND SEAR MECHANISM

COCK

SEAR PIN

SPRING

SEAR

PIVOT

TRIGGER

SNAPHAUNCE

FLINTLOCK

PAN

FRIZZEN

COCK

MAINSPRING

TUMBLER

SEAR

BRIDLE

TRIGGER

Acknowledgements

The publishers are grateful to the following for kindly supplying photographs and for permission to reproduce them: Metropolitan Museum of Art, New York, 5 right, 12; Ministry of Public Building and Works, London, 4, 5 left, 6, 10, 11, 16, 18, 20, 22, 24, 26, 28, 29 bottom, 40, 41, 42, 55, 58; Musée de la Chasse et de la Nature, Paris (photo Routhier), 32–33; W. Keith Neal, Esq., 27, 29 top; Nederlands Legermuseum, Leiden, 8; Patrimonio Nacional, Madrid, 13, 15; Sotheby & Co., 39 right, 52–53; Wallace Collection, London, 2, 19, 23, 30, 38, 43, 45, 46, 48, 50, 51.

COUNTRY LIFE COLLECTORS' GUIDES

Series editor Hugh Newbury
Series designer Ian Muggeridge

Published for Country Life Books by
THE HAMLYN PUBLISHING GROUP LIMITED
LONDON · NEW YORK · SYDNEY · TORONTO
Hamlyn House, Feltham, Middlesex, England

FRENCH PISTOLS AND SPORTING GUNS
ISBN 600435946
© The Hamlyn Publishing Group Limited 1972
Printed in Great Britain by Butler & Tanner Limited, Frome and London